Preface

The study of algorithms is fundamental to the field of computer science and engineering, and it forms the backbone of software development, data processing, and problem-solving. The course **MCS-231: Mobile Computing**, offered by the Indira Gandhi National Open University (IGNOU), is pivotal for students pursuing a degree in computer science. The rigorous curriculum of this course requires students to not only understand the theoretical aspects of algorithms but also to apply this knowledge in solving complex computational problems. To assist students in their journey of mastering this subject, this book presents a comprehensive collection of previous years' unsolved papers of the MCS-231 course. The rationale behind compiling these unsolved papers is to provide students with a valuable resource that will enhance their understanding of the subject and prepare them effectively for examinations. These papers serve as an essential tool for self-assessment, allowing students to gauge their knowledge, identify areas that require further study, and practice solving problems within the time constraints typically imposed by examinations. Moreover, working through these papers helps students develop the analytical thinking and problem-solving skills necessary to excel in the field of Mobile Computing.

This book is meticulously organized to cater to the needs of students at various levels of understanding. Each paper included in this compilation is carefully selected from different years to represent a broad spectrum of topics covered in the MCS-231 syllabus. The problems range from basic algorithmic challenges to more complex scenarios that test a student's ability to design efficient and effective algorithms. By attempting these unsolved papers, students will not only reinforce their theoretical knowledge but also gain hands-on experience in tackling real-world algorithmic problems. In addition to serving as an academic resource, this book is also intended to instil confidence in students as they prepare for their examinations. The exposure to a variety of problems will familiarize students with the types of questions that are likely to appear in exams, enabling them to approach their studies with a strategic mindset. This book encourages a deeper exploration of the subject, prompting students to engage with the material beyond the standard textbook content and to think critically about the design and analysis of algorithms.

We would like to express our gratitude to the students and educators who have contributed to the development of this book. Their insights and feedback have been invaluable in ensuring that this compilation meets the highest standards of academic excellence. As you embark on your journey through the world of algorithms, we hope that this book will be a reliable companion in your studies, helping you to unlock the full potential of your capabilities in the field of computer science.

MCS-231
Master In Computer Application (MCA)
Chapter 1: Term-End Examination, December, 2022
MCS-231: Mobile Computing

Time: 3 Hours
Maximum Marks: 100

Note: Question No. *1* is compulsory and carries 40 marks. Attempt any *three* questions from the rest

1.(a) What is Frequency Division Multiplexing (FDM)? What are its advantages, disadvantages and applications?

Answer: Frequency Division Multiplexing (FDM) is a technique used to combine multiple signals into a single channel by assigning a different frequency band to each signal. Each signal is modulated onto a different carrier frequency, allowing simultaneous transmission without interference.
Advantages of FDM:
- **Efficient Utilization of Bandwidth:** By dividing the available bandwidth into separate channels, FDM allows multiple signals to be transmitted simultaneously.
- **Reduced Interference:** Each signal occupies a distinct frequency band, minimizing the chances of interference.
- **Established Technology:** FDM is a well-known and widely used method in various communication systems, particularly in broadcasting.

Disadvantages of FDM:
- **Bandwidth Limitation:** The number of channels is limited by the available bandwidth; if the demand for channels exceeds this, it can lead to congestion.
- **Complexity in Design:** Implementing FDM systems requires careful design to manage frequency allocation and avoid interference.
- **Cost:** The equipment needed for FDM can be more expensive compared to simpler multiplexing techniques.

Applications of FDM:
- **Television Broadcasting:** FDM is used to transmit multiple TV channels over a single cable or broadcast frequency.
- **Radio Broadcasting:** Different radio stations can operate on different frequencies simultaneously.
- **Telephone Networks:** FDM allows multiple calls to be carried over a single physical line.

(b) What is GPRS? Explain its features. Also, list the services offered by it. 10

Answer: General Packet Radio Service (GPRS) is a mobile data service available to users of GSM mobile phones. It provides data transmission via the existing GSM infrastructure using packet-switched technology, which makes it more efficient for transferring data compared to earlier technologies.
Features of GPRS:
- **Packet Switching:** GPRS uses packet-switching for data transmission, which allows the network resources to be used efficiently by sending data in small packets.
- **Always-On Connectivity:** GPRS enables an always-on connection, meaning that users do not need to dial in each time they want to access the internet.
- **Higher Data Rates:** GPRS can offer data rates from 56 kbps up to 114 kbps, which is faster than traditional GSM.
- **Efficient Data Usage:** GPRS charges are based on the volume of data sent and received rather than the duration of connection, making it cost-effective.
- **Mobility and Seamless Handoff:** It supports mobility, allowing users to stay connected while moving across different networks without interruption.

Services Offered by GPRS:

Web Browsing: GPRS enables mobile web browsing, allowing users to access websites on their mobile devices.
Email Services: Users can send and receive emails over mobile devices.
Multimedia Messaging Service (MMS): GPRS supports the transmission of multimedia messages that include text, pictures, and videos.
Internet Access: Users can access the internet for a variety of services, including social media, online banking, and streaming.
Location-Based Services: GPRS is used for applications like GPS, which provide real-time location-based services.

(c) What is LTE? Explain its features. 10

Answer: **Long-Term Evolution (LTE)** is a 4G wireless broadband technology that provides high-speed data transfer for mobile devices. It is the successor of 3G and provides much faster internet speeds and better performance.
Features of LTE:
- **High Data Speeds:** LTE supports download speeds up to 300 Mbps and upload speeds up to 75 Mbps, making it much faster than previous technologies.
- **Low Latency:** LTE reduces the delay (latency) in data transmission, making real-time applications like video calls and gaming much smoother.
- **All-IP Network:** LTE operates on an all-IP network, which means both voice and data are transmitted over the internet protocol, making it more efficient.
- **Scalability:** LTE can be deployed in different frequency bands and supports a wide range of spectrum bandwidths, allowing for flexible implementation.
- **Multiple Antenna Technology:** LTE uses MIMO (Multiple Input, Multiple Output) technology, which improves data transfer rates and signal quality by using multiple antennas for transmission and reception.

(d) Write a short note on the Ad hoc Networks. 10
Answer: **Ad hoc Networks** are decentralized wireless networks that do not rely on a fixed infrastructure such as routers or access points. In these networks, each device (or node) in the network communicates directly with other devices, forming a self-configuring and self-healing network.
Features of Ad hoc Networks:
- **No Fixed Infrastructure:** Ad hoc networks operate without a central administration or pre-existing infrastructure.
- **Dynamic Topology:** The network topology can change frequently, as nodes are free to move and connect or disconnect from the network at any time.
- **Peer-to-Peer Communication:** Devices communicate directly with each other without needing a central point of control.
- **Self-Configuring:** The network can automatically adjust its configuration as devices enter or leave the network.
- **Resource Sharing:** Nodes in the network can share resources like bandwidth, processing power, or storage.

Applications of Ad hoc Networks:
- **Military Communication:** Used in battlefield communications where infrastructure might be unavailable.
- **Emergency Situations:** Useful in disaster recovery scenarios where traditional networks may be down.
Sensor Networks: Employed in sensor-based environments for gathering and transmitting data.

2. (a) What is a cellular network? Explain its various components. 10

Answer: A **cellular network** is a communication network where the last link is wireless, and the network is distributed over land areas called cells, each served by at least one fixed-location transceiver (usually a base station).

Components of a Cellular Network:

1. Mobile Station (MS): This is the user's device, such as a smartphone, which connects to the network to send and receive data.

2. Base Station (BS): The base station consists of the antenna and transceiver that communicate with the mobile station. It handles radio communication.

3. Cell: Each base station covers a geographical area called a cell. Cells overlap to provide continuous coverage.

4. Mobile Switching Centre (MSC): This is the central component of the network that handles call routing, mobility management, and handover when a user moves from one cell to another.

5. Public Switched Telephone Network (PSTN): The MSC connects calls to the external network, such as the traditional telephone network.

6. Backhaul Network: Connects base stations to the core network for data transmission and coordination.

(b) Explain mobile computing architecture with the help of a diagram. 10

Answer: Mobile Computing Architecture refers to the structure that allows for mobile devices to access applications and services over wireless communication. It consists of multiple layers, which enable seamless interaction between the client (mobile devices) and the server (backend infrastructure).

Components of Mobile Computing Architecture:

1. Mobile Device Layer: This includes the hardware and software components of mobile devices (e.g., smartphones) that interact with applications.

2. Network Layer: Wireless networks such as 4G/5G, Wi-Fi, or Bluetooth connect the mobile devices to the internet and other services.

3. Server Layer: The backend infrastructure (servers) hosts applications, processes data, and provides services to the mobile devices.

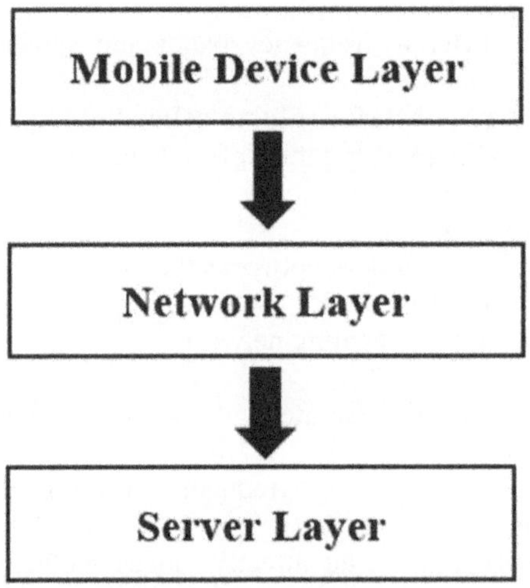

3. (a) List any five applications of mobile computing. 10

Answer: Five applications of mobile computing are:

- **Mobile Banking:** Users can perform banking transactions such as checking balances, transferring money, and paying bills via mobile devices.
- **Navigation and GPS:** Mobile devices offer real-time navigation using GPS to guide users to destinations.
- **Social Networking:** Mobile computing enables users to connect and share content on platforms like Facebook, Twitter, and Instagram.
- **E-commerce:** Mobile applications allow users to shop online, make purchases, and track deliveries.
- **Healthcare:** Mobile devices are used in healthcare for remote monitoring of patients and health data transmission.

(b) Explain J2EE architecture. 10

Answer: Java 2 Platform, Enterprise Edition (J2EE) is a platform designed for building distributed, multi-tiered applications. The architecture consists of multiple layers, enabling the development of scalable, secure, and maintainable enterprise-level applications.

Components of J2EE Architecture:
1. Client Layer: The topmost layer where users interact with the application. This could be a web browser or a mobile app.
2. Web Layer: Contains web components like Servlets and Java Server Pages (JSP), which handle user requests and responses.
3. Business Layer: Includes Enterprise JavaBeans (EJB) that encapsulate the business logic of the application.
4. Data Layer: This layer is responsible for managing database operations and connecting the application to data sources.

4. (a) Explain the functions of a mobile operating system. 10
Answer: A **mobile operating system (OS)** manages the hardware and software resources on a mobile device and provides a platform for applications.
Functions of a Mobile OS:
- **Resource Management:** Allocates memory, processing power, and other resources to applications.
- **User Interface (UI) Management:** Manages the interaction between the user and the device through touchscreens, gestures, etc.
- **Security Management:** Provides security features such as encryption, authentication, and protection against malware.
- **File System Management:** Manages storage of data and file systems on the device.
- **Multitasking:** Allows multiple applications to run simultaneously, efficiently switching between them.

(b) Explain the features of an integrated development platform for mobile apps. 10

Answer: An **Integrated Development Platform (IDP)** for mobile apps provides tools and features that help developers build, test, and deploy mobile applications.
Features:
- **Cross-Platform Development:** Allows developers to create apps for multiple platforms (iOS, Android) using a single code.
- **Emulators and Simulators:** Provides virtual devices to test apps on different platforms without physical devices.
- **Debugging Tools:** Includes features to identify and fix errors in the app during development.
- **UI Design Tools:** Provides drag-and-drop interfaces for designing user interfaces without coding.
- **Integrated Libraries:** Offers pre-built libraries and frameworks that simplify app development.

5. (a) Explain the features of iOS. 10
Answer: iOS is Apple's mobile operating system specifically designed for devices like iPhones and iPads. It is known for its smooth performance, security, and wide range of applications.
Features of iOS:
- **User Interface (UI):** iOS has a simple, clean, and intuitive interface that is easy to use, making it popular among users. It supports multi-touch gestures, swipe, tap, and pinch actions.
- **App Store Integration:** iOS has a vast ecosystem of applications available via the App Store, with rigorous quality control to ensure high standards for apps.
- **Strong Security:** iOS is known for its security features like **Face ID**, **Touch ID**, and **end-to-end encryption**. It regularly provides security updates and restricts access to critical system areas, protecting user data.
- **Seamless Ecosystem:** iOS devices work seamlessly with other Apple products like MacBooks, iPads, and Apple Watches. Features like **Airdrop**, **Handoff**, and **iCloud** ensure easy sharing and synchronization of data between devices.

- **Efficient Multitasking:** iOS allows efficient multitasking, enabling users to switch between multiple apps without affecting performance or battery life.
- **Regular Updates:** Apple provides regular software updates that introduce new features and security patches, ensuring that even older devices remain up-to-date.
- **Siri Integration:** iOS includes **Siri**, a voice assistant that allows users to perform tasks using voice commands, such as setting reminders, sending texts, or checking the weather.
- **iCloud Services:** iOS includes **iCloud**, a cloud storage solution that allows users to store and back up photos, files, and settings. It also provides seamless access to files across devices.
- **Privacy Controls:** iOS offers granular privacy controls, allowing users to manage which apps have access to their location, contacts, and other sensitive data.
- **Augmented Reality (AR):** iOS supports augmented reality applications, with features like **ARKit**, enabling developers to build immersive AR experiences.

(b) Explain the features of XML. 10

Answer: Extensible Markup Language (XML) is a flexible text format used for structuring, storing, and transporting data. It is platform-independent and allows data to be shared across different systems in a consistent way.

Features of XML:
- **Self-Descriptive:** XML is a self-descriptive language, meaning that the tags used in XML files define the structure and meaning of the data. This makes it easy to understand without additional information.
- **Platform-Independent:** XML is platform-independent, meaning it can be used on any device or operating system, making it ideal for data exchange between different systems.
- **Human-Readable:** XML files are plain text, making them easy for humans to read and understand. This is useful for debugging and data verification.
- **Hierarchical Structure:** XML represents data in a tree-like structure, which allows for complex data relationships to be easily modelled. Each element can have nested sub-elements, attributes, and values.
- **Custom Tags:** Unlike HTML, XML allows the creation of custom tags. This flexibility allows users to define their own data structures as needed, giving it an advantage in applications that require specific data formats.
- **Extensibility:** XML can be easily extended as needed by adding new tags without disrupting the existing structure, making it a highly adaptable format.
- **Data Validation:** XML supports schema definitions such as **XML Schema** and **Document Type Definition (DTD)**, which help ensure the correctness and structure of the data.
- **Interoperability:** XML is widely supported by many technologies and programming languages, making it easy to integrate into various systems, including web services and APIs.
- **Separation of Data and Presentation:** XML separates data from its presentation, meaning that the data can be used in multiple ways, such as displaying it on a web page or storing it in a database.
- **Unicode Support:** XML supports Unicode, enabling it to handle data in different languages and scripts, making it ideal for global applications.

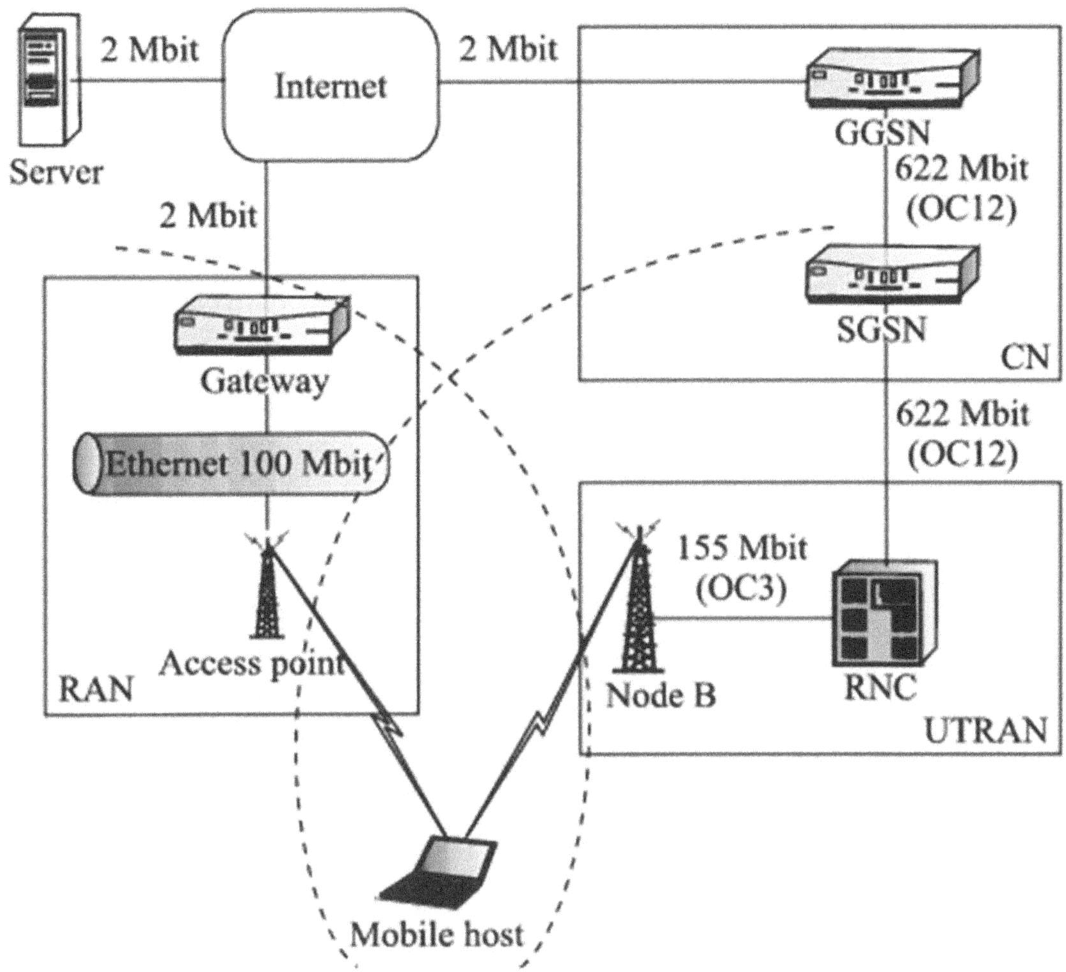
2 Mbit
Internet
2 Mbit
Server
GGSN
622 Mbit
(OC12)
2 Mbit
SGSN
Gateway
CN
Ethernet 100 Mbit
622 Mbit
(OC12)
155 Mbit
(OC3)
Access point
RAN
Node B
RNC
UTRAN
Mobile host

MCS-231
Master In Computer Application (MCA)
Chapter 2: Term-End Examination, June, 2023
MCS-231: Mobile Computing

Time: 3 Hours
Maximum Marks: 100

Note: Question No. *1* is compulsory and carries 40 marks. Attempt any *three* questions from the rest.

1. (a) What is Time Division Multiplexing (TDM)? What are the advantages, disadvantages and applications? 10

Answer: Time Division Multiplexing (TDM) is a method of transmitting multiple signals over a single communication channel by dividing the time frame into several time slots. Each signal gets its dedicated time slot to transmit its data sequentially. TDM ensures that data from different sources is sent without overlapping.
Advantages of TDM:
- **Efficient Bandwidth Utilization:** TDM uses available bandwidth efficiently by assigning each signal its own time slot.
- **No Interference:** Since each signal is transmitted at a different time, there is no interference between them.
- **Flexibility:** It is flexible and can be used in both wired and wireless communication systems.
- **Easy to Implement:** TDM is relatively easy to implement and manage as each signal uses the same frequency but different times.
- **Cost-Effective:** It reduces the need for multiple transmission lines, thus lowering infrastructure costs.

Disadvantages of TDM:
- **Synchronization Issues:** TDM requires precise synchronization to ensure that each signal gets its time slot correctly.
- **Latency:** If the number of users increases, latency can be an issue because each user has to wait for their time slot.
- **Idle Slots:** In some cases, if a user has no data to send, their time slot remains idle, leading to inefficient use of bandwidth.
- **High Overhead:** TDM requires overhead in terms of time synchronization and framing.

Applications of TDM:
- **Telephone Systems:** TDM is widely used in telephone networks to combine multiple voice channels on a single transmission path.
- **Digital TV Broadcasting:** TDM is used to transmit multiple TV channels over a single frequency.
- **Satellite Communication:** TDM is employed in satellite systems to transmit multiple data streams in different time slots.
- **Data Communication:** It is also used in computer networks to allow several devices to share a common communication link.

(b) What is GSM technology? Explain its advantages and disadvantages. 10

Answer: GSM (Global System for Mobile Communications) is a standard developed to describe the protocols for second-generation (2G) mobile networks. It is widely used across the globe for mobile telephony and data services.
Advantages of GSM:
- **Widespread Coverage:** GSM is used in more than 210 countries, making it the most widely adopted mobile technology.

- **International Roaming:** GSM supports international roaming, allowing users to use their mobile phones in different countries.
- **Efficient Spectrum Utilization:** GSM efficiently uses the available spectrum with technologies like **Frequency Division Duplexing (FDD)**.
- **Secure Communication:** GSM provides encryption to secure calls and data transfers, enhancing privacy.
- **SIM Card Flexibility:** GSM uses SIM cards, allowing users to switch devices without changing their phone number or data plan.

Disadvantages of GSM:

- **Limited Data Speed:** GSM is a 2G technology and provides slower data speeds compared to modern technologies like 3G, 4G, or 5G.
- **Interference Issues:** GSM can experience interference in areas with many other electronic devices operating on the same frequencies.
- **Lower Voice Quality:** The voice quality in GSM networks is often lower compared to more advanced technologies.
- **Spectrum Congestion:** In densely populated areas, GSM networks can face congestion, leading to call drops or delays.

(c) What is a 4G network? Explain its features. 10

Answer: 4G (Fourth Generation) network is the successor to 3G, offering significantly faster data transfer rates and enhanced network capabilities. 4G networks enable high-speed internet access, HD streaming, and other advanced mobile services.

Features of a 4G Network:

- **High Data Transfer Rates:** 4G offers speeds of up to 100 Mbps for mobile devices and 1 Gbps for stationary devices.
- **Low Latency:** 4G networks have low latency, which is critical for applications like online gaming, video conferencing, and real-time data streaming.
- **IP-Based Network:** 4G is entirely based on **Internet Protocol (IP)**, allowing seamless integration with the internet and supporting voice-over-IP (VoIP) calls.
- **Enhanced Multimedia Services:** 4G supports HD video streaming, video conferencing, and advanced mobile TV services.
- **Support for Mobility:** 4G provides consistent high-speed internet even when users are on the move, ideal for transportation systems like trains and buses.
- **Security:** It offers enhanced security features like **IPSec** and advanced encryption methods to secure data communication.

- **Multitasking:** Users can make voice calls, send texts, and browse the internet simultaneously.
- **Better Spectrum Efficiency:** 4G uses **Orthogonal Frequency Division Multiplexing (OFDM)** to enhance spectrum efficiency, allowing more data to be transmitted over the same bandwidth.

(d) What is WIMAX? Explain its features. 10

Answer: WiMAX (Worldwide Interoperability for Microwave Access) is a wireless communication standard designed to provide high-speed internet access over long distances. It can serve both mobile and fixed internet users and is considered a competitor to LTE.

Features of WiMAX:

- **Long-Range Coverage:** WiMAX can cover large areas, with a range of up to 50 kilometres (31 miles) for fixed stations and 5-15 kilometres (3-9 miles) for mobile stations.
- **High Data Speeds:** WiMAX supports data speeds of up to 70 Mbps, which allows for high-speed broadband internet access.
- **Supports Mobility:** WiMAX enables users to remain connected while on the move, making it suitable for mobile broadband services.
- **Scalable Bandwidth:** WiMAX offers flexible bandwidth allocations, allowing service providers to allocate resources as per user demand.

- **Quality of Service (QoS):** It provides a robust Quality of Service (QoS) mechanism that ensures smooth delivery of voice, video, and data services.
- **Broad Spectrum:** WiMAX can operate in various frequency bands (2.3 GHz to 3.5 GHz), providing flexibility in deployment.
- **Interoperability:** WiMAX is designed to be interoperable with other wireless technologies, making it easy for devices from different manufacturers to work together.
- **Cost-Effective:** WiMAX is considered cost-effective for providing broadband in areas where wired connections are difficult to deploy, such as rural or remote regions.

2.(a) What is Data Synchronization? Explain it. 10

Answer: Data Synchronization is the process of ensuring that data is consistent, up-to-date, and identical across multiple systems, devices, or databases. It involves the exchange and harmonization of data so that all participating devices or systems reflect the same information at any given point in time. In the context of mobile devices, data synchronization ensures that data on a smartphone, for example, matches the data stored on cloud servers, computers, or other devices.

How Data Synchronization Works:
- **Two-way Sync:** This involves both the sending and receiving of data, where changes made on either the device or server are updated across all platforms.
- **One-way Sync:** Data flows in one direction, either from the server to the device or from the device to the server.
- **Conflict Resolution:** When data changes in multiple places, a conflict resolution mechanism decides which version of the data is most recent or most accurate.

Types of Data Synchronization:
- **Real-time Synchronization:** Data is updated across systems instantly as changes are made.
- **Scheduled Synchronization:** Data is synchronized at set intervals, ensuring that devices stay up-to-date without needing constant connection.
- **Manual Synchronization:** Users manually trigger synchronization between devices or systems.

Importance of Data Synchronization:
- **Consistency:** Ensures that all devices and systems reflect the same information, eliminating discrepancies.
- **Convenience:** Allows users to access the latest version of their data from any device or platform.
- **Backup:** Helps in creating backups of data, so if one device is lost or damaged, the data can still be accessed elsewhere.

Applications of Data Synchronization:
- **Cloud Storage Services:** Google Drive, iCloud, and Dropbox use data synchronization to ensure that the files stored in the cloud are the same as those on the local device.
- **Email Services:** Email services synchronize your inbox across multiple devices, ensuring you have access to the same emails regardless of where you check them.
- **Enterprise Systems:** Businesses use synchronization tools to ensure that data from different departments, branches, or mobile users is harmonized and up-to-date in central databases.

(b) Write a short note on Mobile Commerce. 10

Answer: Mobile Commerce (m-commerce) refers to the buying and selling of goods and services through wireless handheld devices such as smartphones and tablets. It is a sub-category of electronic commerce (e-commerce) that leverages the capabilities of mobile devices to enable transactions over the internet.

Key Features of Mobile Commerce:
- **Convenience:** Users can engage in shopping, banking, and other transactions from virtually anywhere, making it highly convenient.
- **Mobile Payments:** M-commerce allows users to make payments directly from their mobile devices using methods like mobile wallets (e.g., Google Pay, Apple Pay) and mobile banking apps.

- **Location-Based Services:** M-commerce often integrates location-based services (GPS) to offer personalized deals, recommendations, or services based on the user's geographical location.
- **Mobile Apps:** Many companies create dedicated mobile applications to enhance user experience and provide a streamlined shopping experience.
- **Instant Connectivity:** Mobile devices allow constant connectivity, enabling businesses to engage with customers 24/7.

Types of Mobile Commerce:
- **Mobile Banking:** Users can access their bank accounts, transfer money, and manage their finances through banking apps.
- **Mobile Shopping:** E-commerce platforms like Amazon, Flipkart, and eBay have mobile apps allowing users to browse, purchase, and track products directly from their phones.
- **Mobile Ticketing:** Users can purchase tickets for movies, events, flights, and public transportation using mobile apps.
- **Mobile Wallets and Payments:** Mobile wallets like Paytm, PhonePe, and Apple Pay enable users to make secure online and in-store payments.
- **Mobile Marketing and Advertising:** Businesses can send promotional messages or ads directly to users' smartphones, often targeting specific audiences based on their browsing habits or location.

Advantages of Mobile Commerce:
- **Accessibility:** Consumers can access products, services, and information at any time, increasing flexibility.
- **Personalization:** M-commerce enables businesses to deliver personalized experiences based on users' browsing history, preferences, and location.
- **Instant Notifications:** Users can receive instant alerts about deals, offers, and other important information through push notifications.

Disadvantages of Mobile Commerce:
- **Security Risks:** M-commerce involves transferring sensitive information like banking details, making it susceptible to cyber threats.
- **Device Dependency:** A mobile device's functionality and limitations, like small screen size or battery life, can affect the user experience.
- **Technical Challenges:** Connectivity issues or app bugs can disrupt the m-commerce experience.

3. (a) Draw and explain Android architecture. 10

Answer: Android Architecture consists of several layers, each providing essential services and functionalities to the system. The architecture is designed in such a way that it supports mobile devices with limited resources while providing a rich user experience.

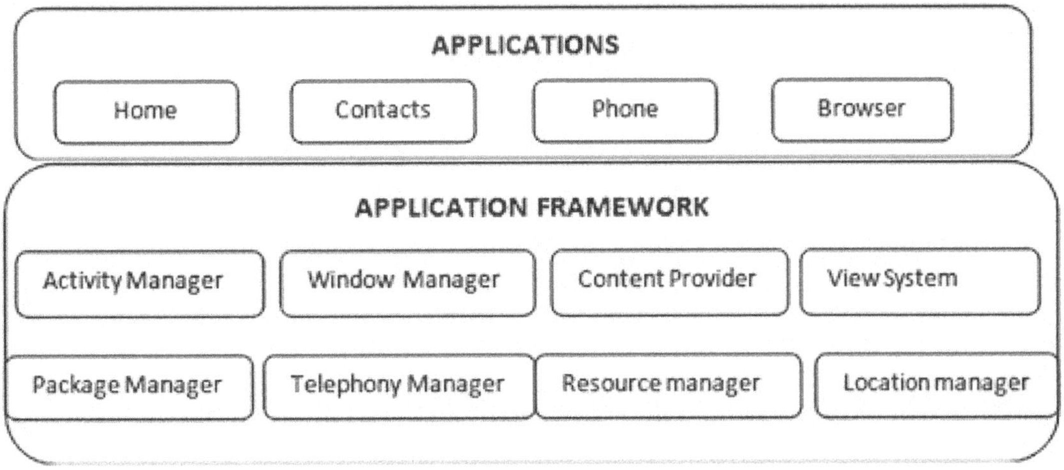

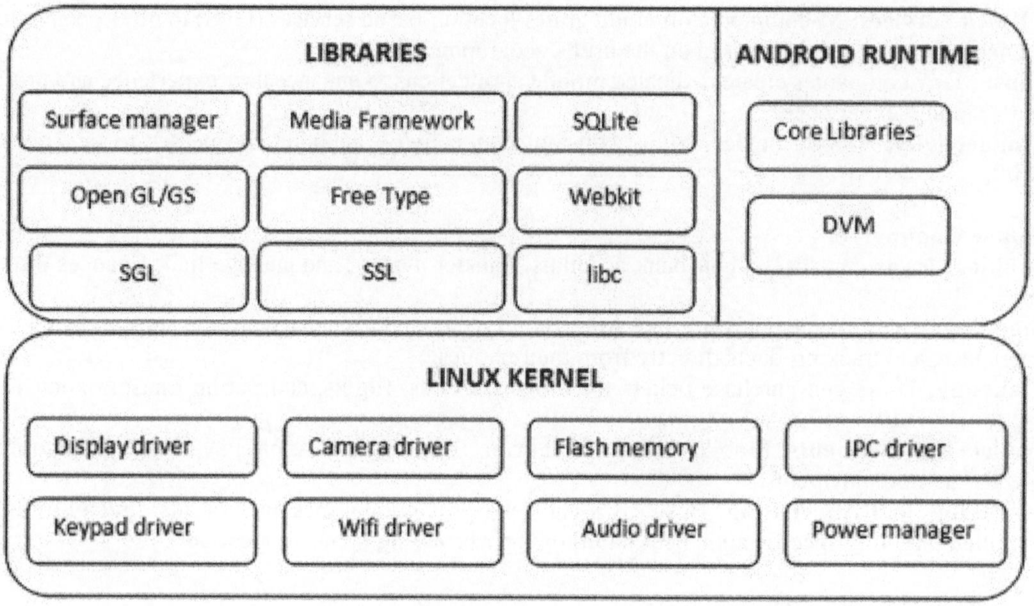

Here is an explanation of the key layers in Android Architecture:

1. Linux Kernel: The base layer of the Android architecture is the Linux Kernel. It acts as an abstraction layer between the hardware and the rest of the software stack. The Linux kernel is responsible for managing core services such as:

- Memory management
- Process management
- Security settings
- Power management
- Hardware drivers (for display, camera, Wi-Fi, Bluetooth, etc.)

2. Hardware Abstraction Layer (HAL): HAL provides standard interfaces for the hardware components, allowing Android to interact with different hardware without needing to know the low-level implementation details. It simplifies communication between the Android framework and device hardware.

3. Native Libraries: Above the kernel, Android includes a set of native libraries written in C/C++ that support various features like graphics rendering, media playback, and database management. Some key libraries include:

- **Surface Manager:** Manages access to the display subsystem.
- **OpenGL/ES:** Provides 2D and 3D graphics rendering.
- **SQLite:** A lightweight relational database for storage purposes.
- **WebKit:** Used for web browsing functionality.

4. Android Runtime (ART): ART is the environment in which Android applications run. It includes the core Java libraries and provides the necessary support for executing Android applications. Key components of ART:

- **Garbage Collector (GC):** Automatically manages memory allocation and deallocation.
- **Dex Bytecode Interpreter:** Executes the bytecode format known as Dalvik Executable (.dex), which is optimized for mobile environments.

5. Application Framework: The Application Framework layer provides higher-level services for app development. Developers use these APIs to build applications. Some key components include:

- **Activity Manager:** Manages the lifecycle of apps and provides a navigational stack.
- **Content Providers:** Manages data sharing between applications.
- **Location Manager:** Provides access to location services such as GPS.
- **Resource Manager:** Manages application resources like strings, layouts, and graphics.

6. Applications: The top layer of the Android architecture is the application layer. All apps, whether system or third-party apps, are built using the same APIs. Examples include the camera app, messaging app, phone dealer, etc.

(b) Explain various components of J2ME. 10

Answer: J2ME (Java 2 Micro Edition) is a technology specifically designed for developing applications for mobile and embedded devices with limited resources. The components of J2ME are structured in a way to accommodate the varying requirements of different devices.

The main components of J2ME include:

- **Configurations:** Configurations define the basic Java runtime environment for a particular category of devices. It specifies the Java Virtual Machine (JVM), the libraries, and the core functionalities available for the applications.
- **Connected Limited Device Configuration (CLDC):** Designed for small devices with limited processing power and memory (e.g., mobile phones). CLDC includes a subset of the Java standard libraries.
- **Connected Device Configuration (CDC):** Used for more powerful devices such as set-top boxes and high-end PDAs. CDC provides a more extensive set of Java libraries compared to CLDC.
- **Profiles:** Profiles are built on top of configurations and provide additional APIs for specific types of devices. Profiles determine the application lifecycle, user interface, and other key functionalities.
- **Mobile Information Device Profile (MIDP):** The most widely used profile for mobile phones. It adds features like a user interface, persistent storage, and networking capabilities to CLDC.
- **Foundation Profile:** Designed for devices that require a higher level of functionality, typically used in conjunction with CDC.
- **Optional Packages:** Optional packages are extensions to the core profiles that provide extra functionalities. These packages allow the customization of applications for specific hardware or software environments. Examples include:

Wireless Messaging API (WMA): Allows applications to send and receive SMS and MMS messages.

Mobile Media API (MMAPI): Provides multimedia support, allowing the creation of audio, video, and image-based applications.

- **Java Virtual Machine (JVM):** J2ME uses a JVM designed for resource-constrained environments. The JVM interprets bytecode and executes it on the device. In J2ME, there are two main types of JVM:

KVM (Kilobyte Virtual Machine): **Used in CLDC and is optimized for devices with small memory footprints.**

CVM (Compact Virtual Machine): **Used in CDC and designed for more powerful devices.**

MIDlet's: **MIDlet's** are applications built using the MIDP profile. They define the application lifecycle (starting, pausing, and destroying the app). MIDlet are deployed in .JAR files and can run on any device that supports the MIDP profile.

3. (a) What is guided transmission? How does it differ from unguided transmission? Give example(s). 10

Answer: Guided transmission refers to the method of transmitting data signals through physical paths such as cables or optical fibres. It requires a well-defined medium for signal transmission, where the signals are directed along specific paths. Guided transmission is commonly used for short-range communication and within specific networks, such as LANs.

Examples of guided transmission media:

- **Twisted Pair Cable:** Used in telecommunication networks and Ethernet connections.
- **Coaxial Cable:** Used for cable television and internet connections.
- **Optical Fiber:** Used for high-speed data transmission over long distances, offering high bandwidth and low signal attenuation.

Unguided transmission, on the other hand, refers to the transmission of signals through free space without using a physical medium. Instead, signals are transmitted through air or vacuum using electromagnetic waves. This type of transmission is used for wireless communication, such as satellite, cellular, and radio frequency communication.

Examples of unguided transmission media:

- **Radio Waves:** Used in mobile phones, AM/FM radios, and Wi-Fi.
- **Microwaves:** Used for satellite communication and point-to-point connections.

- **Infrared Waves:** Used for short-range communication such as remote controls.
Differences between guided and unguided transmission:

Parameter	Guided Transmission	Unguided Transmission
Medium	Uses a physical medium (cables, optical fiber)	Uses wireless medium (air, vacuum)
Distance	Suitable for short to medium distances	Suitable for long distances (e.g., satellite)
Signal Quality	Generally, less prone to interference	More prone to interference from external sources
Bandwidth	High bandwidth, especially with optical fiber	Limited bandwidth compared to guided media
Cost	Higher installation cost due to the need for physical cabling	Lower installation cost for large areas (e.g., Wi-Fi, satellite)

(b) Explain any two reasons for weakening of figural strength after transmission. 10

Answer: Signal weakening, also known as **attenuation**, refers to the reduction in signal strength as it travels through a medium. Two primary reasons for signal weakening after transmission are:

Attenuation due to Distance:

As signals travel over long distances, their strength naturally diminishes. The energy in the signal dissipates over time, leading to reduced amplitude and clarity by the time it reaches the receiver. This is particularly noticeable in guided transmission media like twisted pair cables, where resistance in the wire can cause significant energy loss.

Interference from External Sources:

External electromagnetic sources can cause interference, resulting in a decrease in the signal's strength and quality. This is especially common in unguided transmission, where radio waves and microwaves are subject to interference from other signals, electrical noise, and environmental factors like weather or obstacles (buildings, trees). In wireless communication, interference can significantly degrade signal quality, leading to loss of data or the need for retransmission.

4.(a) What is an antenna? What is its functionality? On what factor(s) does its size depend on? 10

Answer: **Antenna** is a device used to transmit and receive electromagnetic signals, particularly radio waves, for communication purposes. It acts as an interface between the radio wave propagation environment and the electronic devices, such as radios, mobile phones, or satellite communication systems.

Functionality of an Antenna:

- **Transmission:** In transmission mode, the antenna converts electrical signals from the transmitter into electromagnetic waves and radiates them into the surrounding environment.
- **Reception:** In reception mode, the antenna captures electromagnetic waves from the environment and converts them into electrical signals to be processed by the receiver.

Antennas are essential in wireless communication systems such as cellular networks, satellite communication, Wi-Fi, and broadcasting systems.

Factors Affecting Antenna Size:

Wavelength of the Signal:

- The size of the antenna is primarily dependent on the wavelength (λ) of the electromagnetic wave it needs to transmit or receive. Generally, the length of the antenna is proportional to the wavelength of the signal. The most common types of antennas are designed as a fraction (e.g., half or quarter) of the signal's wavelength.
- **Formula:** Antenna Length ≈ **λ2** (for a half-wave dipole antenna).
- For example, lower frequency signals (longer wavelength) require larger antennas, while higher frequency signals (shorter wavelength) use smaller antennas.

Frequency of Operation:

- Antenna size is inversely proportional to the operating frequency. Higher frequencies (shorter wavelengths) allow for smaller antennas, while lower frequencies require larger antennas.
- **Relationship:** Antenna Size$\propto$1/Frequency

Type of Antenna: Different antenna designs (e.g., dipole, Yagi, parabolic, or patch antennas) have different size requirements based on their specific applications and intended use in transmitting and receiving signals.

(b) What is CDMA? How does it differ from GSM? 10

Answer: CDMA (Code Division Multiple Access) is a digital communication technology that allows multiple users to share the same frequency spectrum by assigning unique codes to each user. It uses spread-spectrum technology, where signals are spread over a wide frequency range using distinct codes, making it possible for many users to occupy the same channel without interference.
Functionality of CDMA:
- In CDMA, each user is assigned a unique spreading code, which allows their signals to be distinguished from others on the same frequency. The receiver uses the same code to reconstruct the original signal, filtering out other signals as noise.

How CDMA Differs from GSM:

Parameter	CDMA (Code Division Multiple Access)	GSM (Global System for Mobile Communication)
Technology	CDMA assigns unique codes to each user to separate signals on the same frequency.	GSM uses Time Division Multiple Access (TDMA), assigning different time slots to different users on the same frequency.
Frequency Sharing	Users share the same frequency spectrum but are distinguished by unique codes.	Users are allocated specific frequency bands and time slots.
Efficiency	CDMA allows more users to share the same frequency band, improving spectrum efficiency.	GSM limits the number of users per frequency due to time-slot assignment.
Signal Handoff	Soft handoff: CDMA allows seamless transition between cell towers, maintaining connections on multiple towers before switching.	Hard handoff: GSM requires the call to drop the connection from one cell tower before connecting to another.
Data Rate	CDMA can provide higher data rates and better performance in high-traffic areas.	GSM offers moderate data rates, suitable for voice communication and basic data services.
Security	CDMA is inherently more secure due to the spreading codes used, making it difficult to intercept and decode.	GSM security is based on encryption algorithms but can be less secure than CDMA.
Geographical Use	Predominantly used in the USA and some Asian countries.	Widely used across Europe, Asia, Africa, and globally.

MCS-231
Master In Computer Applications (MCA)
Chapter 3: Term-End Examination, December, 2023
MCS-231: Mobile Computing

Time: 3 Hours
Maximum Marks :100

Note: Question No. *1* is compulsory and carries 40 marks. Attempt any *three* questions from the rest.

1.**(a)** What is Time Division Multiplexing (TDM)? What are its advantages, disadvantages and applications? 10

Answer: Time Division Multiplexing (TDM) is a digital multiplexing technique that divides the time on a single communication channel into multiple time slots, allowing multiple signals to share the same channel. Each signal is assigned a specific time slot during which it can transmit its data. TDM is commonly used in both telecommunications and computer networking.
Advantages of TDM:
- **Efficient Use of Bandwidth:** TDM allows multiple signals to share the same bandwidth, maximizing the use of available channel capacity.
- **Elimination of Interference:** Since each signal is assigned a distinct time slot, the risk of interference between signals is minimized.
- **Simplicity in Synchronization:** TDM systems can be designed to maintain synchronization between the transmitter and receiver, ensuring accurate data transmission.
- **Lower Cost:** TDM reduces the need for multiple physical channels, resulting in cost savings for infrastructure.

Disadvantages of TDM:
- **Delay in Transmission:** The time-slot allocation may introduce delays, especially if the number of users increases, leading to longer wait times for transmission.
-**Fixed Bandwidth Allocation:** If a user has no data to send during their allocated time slot, that time is wasted, leading to inefficient bandwidth usage.
- **Complexity in Implementation:** TDM systems can be more complex to design and implement than simple point-to-point connections.

Applications of TDM:
- **Telecommunication Systems:** TDM is widely used in telephone networks for long-distance communication.
- **Digital Signal Processing:** TDM is employed in digital audio and video systems to transmit multiple signals over a single channel.
- **Data Communication:** TDM is used in local area networks (LANs) and other digital communication systems to manage multiple data streams efficiently.

(b) What is a Cellular Network? Under what conditions frequency reuse is possible by different cells in the network 10
Answer: A **cellular network** is a communication network that uses a system of interconnected base stations, or cells, to provide wireless coverage over a large geographical area. Each cell contains a base station that communicates with mobile devices within its coverage area. Cellular networks are designed to enable multiple users to connect and communicate simultaneously without interference.
Conditions for Frequency Reuse in Cellular Networks:
- **Distance Between Cells:** Frequency reuse is possible when there is sufficient distance between cells using the same frequency. The distance must be great enough to prevent signal interference and ensure clear communication.
- **Cellular Layout:** The cellular layout should be designed such that cells using the same frequency are separated by a predetermined distance, which is based on factors like terrain, buildings, and population density.

- **Directional Antennas:** Utilizing directional antennas at base stations can help limit the coverage area of a particular frequency, allowing for more efficient frequency reuse.
- **Low Traffic Areas:** In regions where user demand is low, frequencies can be reused in adjacent cells since the chances of simultaneous usage are reduced.
- **Signal Strength:** Ensuring that the signal strength of cells using the same frequency does not overlap significantly is crucial for minimizing interference.

(c) What are Smart Sensors? What are the instances where mobile devices interact with their surroundings with the help of sensors? 10

Answer: Smart sensors are advanced devices that can collect, process, and communicate data about their environment. They combine sensing elements with processing capabilities, allowing them to perform complex tasks such as data analysis and decision-making without the need for constant external input.

Instances of Mobile Devices Interacting with Their Surroundings Using Sensors:
- **Location-Based Services:** GPS sensors in mobile devices enable users to access location-based services, such as navigation and local search, providing real-time information based on the user's location.
- **Health Monitoring:** Wearable devices equipped with smart sensors can track vital signs like heart rate, temperature, and physical activity, providing users with insights into their health and fitness.
- **Environmental Monitoring:** Sensors can measure environmental conditions such as temperature, humidity, and air quality, allowing mobile devices to provide information about the surroundings.
- **Augmented Reality (AR):** Mobile devices equipped with cameras and motion sensors can interact with their environment to overlay digital information onto the real world, enhancing the user experience in applications such as gaming and education.
- **Smart Home Integration:** Mobile devices can connect with smart sensors in home automation systems to control lighting, heating, and security, allowing users to monitor and manage their home environment remotely.

(d) Write a short note on Mobile Device Database Management. 10

Answer: Mobile Device Database Management refers to the methods and technologies used to store, retrieve, and manage data on mobile devices. With the increasing reliance on mobile applications for business and personal use, efficient database management has become crucial for maintaining performance and user experience.

Key Aspects of Mobile Device Database Management:
- **Local Databases:** Mobile devices often use local databases (e.g., SQLite) to store data locally for quick access and offline functionality. This allows apps to function without a constant internet connection.
- **Remote Databases:** Many mobile applications utilize cloud-based databases (e.g., Firebase, AWS) to store and sync data across devices, ensuring data consistency and accessibility from multiple devices.
- **Data Synchronization:** Synchronization mechanisms are implemented to ensure that local data is updated with the latest changes from the remote database, providing users with real-time data.
- **Data Security:** Mobile database management includes security measures to protect sensitive user data from unauthorized access and data breaches. This may involve encryption and secure authentication methods.
- **Scalability:** Mobile databases must be scalable to accommodate growing amounts of data and an increasing number of users, ensuring consistent performance as the application grows.

2.(a) List various steps in the development of a Mobile App. What are the various components of an Enterprise Mobile Application? 10

Answer: Steps in the Development of a Mobile App:

i. Idea Generation and Research:
- Identify a problem that the app will solve or a need it will fulfil.
- Conduct market research to validate the idea and analyse competitors.

ii. Define Objectives and Requirements:
- Establish clear objectives for the app.
- Determine the target audience and user personas.
- Outline functional and non-functional requirements.

iii. Wireframing and Prototyping:

- Create wireframes to visualize the app's layout and user interface.
- Develop prototypes to demonstrate the app's functionality and gather feedback.

iii. Technology Stack Selection:
- Choose the appropriate technologies for front-end and back-end development.
- Decide whether to develop a native, hybrid, or web app.

iv. Design and User Interface (UI):
- Create the app's visual elements, including colours, typography, and icons.
- Focus on user experience (UX) to ensure intuitive navigation.

v. Development:
- Write the code for the app, integrating necessary features and functionalities.
- Use Agile development methodologies for iterative progress.

vi. Testing:
- Conduct thorough testing, including unit, integration, and user acceptance testing.
- Identify and fix bugs and issues to enhance performance and usability.

vii. Deployment:
- Prepare the app for launch by ensuring compliance with app store guidelines.
- Deploy the app to relevant app stores (e.g., Google Play, Apple App Store).

viii. Marketing and Promotion:
- Create a marketing strategy to promote the app and attract users.
- Utilize social media, blogs, and advertising to generate interest.

ix. Maintenance and Updates:
- Regularly update the app to fix bugs, improve features, and adapt to changing user needs.
- Gather user feedback for continuous improvement.

Components of an Enterprise Mobile Application:

i. User Interface (UI):
- A responsive and user-friendly interface tailored for enterprise users.

ii. Backend Services:
- Integration with backend systems such as databases, APIs, and cloud services for data retrieval and storage.

iii. Security Features:
- Authentication and authorization mechanisms to ensure secure access to sensitive data.
- Data encryption and secure data transmission protocols.

iv. Data Management:
- Efficient data handling, including synchronization with enterprise databases and handling offline access.

v. Business Logic Layer:
- Implementation of core business rules and workflows to ensure alignment with enterprise processes.

vi. Analytics and Reporting:
- Tools for tracking user behaviour and app performance, allowing businesses to make data-driven decisions.

vii. Integration Capabilities:
- Ability to integrate with other enterprise applications (e.g., CRM, ERP) for seamless data flow.

viii. Scalability:
- Capacity to handle increasing loads as the number of users grows, ensuring performance stability.

ix. Notifications:
- Push notification functionality to keep users informed about updates, alerts, and messages.

x. Support and Maintenance:
- Ongoing technical support to address issues and provide updates as needed.

(b) Write a short note on XML. 10

Answer: XML (extensible Markup Language) is a flexible markup language used to store and transport structured data. It is designed to be both human-readable and machine-readable, making it an ideal format for data interchange between systems.

Key Features of XML:

- **Self-Descriptive:** XML allows users to define their own tags, making the data structure self-descriptive. This feature enhances the clarity and understanding of the data.

- **Hierarchical Structure:** XML organizes data in a hierarchical format, with elements nested within one another. This structure makes it easier to represent complex relationships.
- **Platform-Independent:** XML is platform-agnostic, meaning it can be used across different operating systems and applications without compatibility issues.
- **Extensible:** Users can create custom tags to suit their data needs, allowing XML to adapt to various applications and industries.
- **Data Interchange:** XML is widely used for data interchange between web services and applications, facilitating communication between different systems.
- **Support for Unicode:** XML supports Unicode, allowing it to handle a wide range of characters from different languages, making it suitable for international applications.

Applications of XML:
- **Web Services:** XML is commonly used in web services (SOAP and REST) to exchange data between clients and servers.
- **Configuration Files:** Many applications use XML files for configuration settings due to their readability and ease of modification.
- **Data Storage:** XML can be used as a lightweight data storage format for applications needing structured data storage without a full database system.
- **Document Representation:** XML is employed in various document formats, such as XHTML and SVG, for representing structured content.

3. **(a)** What is J2ME? Explain main components of J2ME. 10

Answer: J2ME (Java 2 Micro Edition) is a platform designed for developing applications on small devices, such as mobile phones, PDAs, and embedded systems. It is part of the Java platform and provides a set of APIs and tools specifically tailored for resource-constrained environments. J2ME enables developers to create portable applications that can run on various devices regardless of the manufacturer.
Main Components of J2ME:
- Configuration:
J2ME defines two main configurations, which are the foundation upon which applications are built:
a. CLDC (Connected Limited Device Configuration): Designed for devices with limited resources (low memory and processing power), such as basic mobile phones. It provides a minimal set of Java classes for application development.
b. CDC (Connected Device Configuration): Targeted at more capable devices with greater resources (like set-top boxes and high-end phones). It provides a more extensive set of APIs compared to CLDC.

- Profile:
Profiles are built on top of configurations and provide additional APIs specific to certain device types. The most common profiles are:
a. MIDP (Mobile Information Device Profile): Used in conjunction with CLDC, it offers features for developing mobile applications, including UI components, persistent data storage, and networking capabilities.
b. MHP (Multimedia Home Platform): Designed for interactive digital television and set-top boxes, extending CDC for multimedia applications.

Application Lifecycle:
J2ME applications have a defined lifecycle that includes states such as:
a. Paused: The application is temporarily inactive.
b. Active: The application is currently running and can interact with users.
c. Destroyed: The application is no longer in memory and has been terminated.

User Interface (UI):
J2ME provides a set of UI components that developers can use to create graphical interfaces. These components include forms, lists, and canvas for custom drawing, allowing for a rich user experience despite the constraints of the device.

Persistent Storage:

J2ME supports persistent data storage through the Record Management System (RMS), enabling applications to save user data and settings across sessions.

Networking:
J2ME applications can connect to the internet or other networks using the API provided for HTTP and TCP/IP connections, allowing for data exchange and real-time communication.

Applications of J2ME:
J2ME is widely used for mobile games, messaging applications, location-based services, and various other mobile applications due to its portability and resource-efficient design.

(b) Write a short note on Android. 10

Answer: Android is an open-source mobile operating system developed by Google, designed primarily for touchscreen mobile devices such as smartphones and tablets. Launched in 2008, Android has grown to become the most widely used mobile OS globally, powering a diverse range of devices from various manufacturers.
Key Features of Android:
1. Open Source:
- Android is based on the Linux kernel and is open-source, allowing developers to modify and customize the source code to suit their needs. This encourages innovation and a broad range of applications.
2. User-Friendly Interface:
Android provides an intuitive and user-friendly interface, making it easy for users to navigate and interact with applications. The use of touch gestures and widgets enhances the user experience.
3. Application Framework:
Android offers a rich application framework that enables developers to create feature-rich applications. It includes various APIs for accessing device hardware, such as cameras, GPS, and sensors.
4. Multi-Tasking:
Android supports multi-tasking, allowing users to run multiple applications simultaneously and switch between them seamlessly.
5. Connectivity:
Android devices support various connectivity options, including Wi-Fi, Bluetooth, NFC, and cellular networks, enabling easy access to the internet and other devices.
6. Google Play Store:
The Google Play Store is the primary distribution platform for Android applications. It offers a vast library of apps across different categories, from games to productivity tools.
7. Regular Updates:
Google provides regular updates and security patches for Android, ensuring that devices remain secure and feature-rich.

Applications of Android:
- Android is used for a wide range of applications, including social networking, gaming, productivity, and multimedia. Its versatility and extensive app ecosystem have made it a popular choice for both consumers and developers.

4. (a) Explain the features of integrated development platforms that are used for Mobile App development. 10
Answer: Integrated Development Platforms (IDEs) for mobile app development provide a comprehensive environment for developers to create, test, and deploy mobile applications efficiently. These platforms come with various features that streamline the development process and enhance productivity.
Key Features of Integrated Development Platforms:
- **User-Friendly Interface:** Most IDEs come with a graphical user interface (GUI) that makes it easier for developers to navigate through different tools and functionalities. This interface often includes drag-and-drop capabilities, simplifying the design process for mobile apps.
- **Code Editor:** A powerful code editor is a core feature of any IDE. It typically includes syntax highlighting, code completion, and error detection, helping developers write code more efficiently and reducing the likelihood of bugs.

- **Debugging Tools:** IDEs offer integrated debugging tools that allow developers to test their applications in real-time. These tools help identify and fix errors in the code quickly, making the development process more efficient.
- **Emulators and Simulators:** Integrated development platforms provide emulators or simulators that allow developers to test their apps on various virtual devices without needing physical hardware. This feature helps in verifying the app's performance across different screen sizes and resolutions.
- **Version Control Integration:** Many IDEs support version control systems like Git, allowing developers to manage changes to their code, collaborate with team members, and maintain a history of modifications. This is crucial for team-based development projects.
- **Cross-Platform Development:** Some integrated development platforms support cross-platform development, enabling developers to create applications that run on multiple operating systems (such as Android and iOS) from a single codebase. This feature saves time and resources.
- **Built-in Testing Tools:** Integrated testing frameworks are often included, enabling developers to write and run unit tests, integration tests, and user acceptance tests directly within the IDE. This ensures higher code quality and better performance.
- **Performance Analysis Tools:** Performance analysis tools help developers monitor and optimize their applications for better performance, battery efficiency, and resource management. These tools provide insights into how the app behaves under different conditions.
- **Deployment Support:** IDEs usually provide straightforward deployment options for publishing apps to various app stores. This includes support for packaging, signing, and submitting the application, making it easier for developers to reach their audience.
- **Community Support and Resources:** Many integrated development platforms have large communities that offer tutorials, plugins, and libraries. This support can greatly assist developers in overcoming challenges and learning new skills.

(b) Explain any five features of Mobile Communications. 10

Answer: Mobile Communications refer to the ability to communicate wirelessly using mobile devices, allowing users to connect, share, and exchange information without being tethered to a fixed location. Here are five key features of mobile communications:
- **Mobility:** The most significant feature of mobile communication is mobility. Users can communicate and access information from anywhere within the network coverage area, allowing for seamless connectivity while on the move. This enhances convenience and productivity, making it possible to stay connected regardless of location.
- **Wireless Connectivity:** Mobile communication relies on wireless technologies such as cellular networks, Wi-Fi, and Bluetooth. This eliminates the need for physical cables, enabling users to connect to the internet and other devices wirelessly. Wireless connectivity supports a wide range of applications, including voice calls, text messaging, and data transfer.
- **Data Services:** Mobile communication supports various data services, including internet browsing, email, and multimedia messaging. These services allow users to access information, communicate with others, and share content (like photos and videos) directly from their mobile devices, enhancing the overall user experience.
- **Global Reach:** Mobile communication enables users to connect globally, regardless of geographical barriers. With the help of satellite and cellular networks, individuals can make international calls, send messages, and access online services, facilitating communication across different countries and regions.
- **Diverse Applications:** Mobile communications support a variety of applications, ranging from social media and e-commerce to navigation and health monitoring. The versatility of mobile apps enhances the functionality of mobile devices, allowing users to customize their experience based on personal preferences and needs.

5. (a) Explain the design considerations for Mobile Computing. 10

Answer: Mobile computing involves using wireless devices and networks to communicate and perform tasks while on the move. Designing for mobile computing requires careful consideration of several factors to ensure optimal performance, user experience, and efficient resource utilization.

Key Design Considerations for Mobile Computing:
- **Limited Battery Life:** Mobile devices rely on batteries, and extending battery life is crucial. Developers need to design applications that minimize power consumption by optimizing tasks like background processing, reducing screen brightness, and managing network usage efficiently.

- **Connectivity Issues:** Mobile devices frequently experience changes in network connectivity due to movement across different locations. Designs must handle varying network conditions like weak signals, loss of connection, or transitions between 3G, 4G, Wi-Fi, and other networks. Offline functionality or graceful degradation should be implemented in case of network failure.
- **Small Screen Size and Resolution:** Mobile devices come in various screen sizes, which are much smaller than desktops or laptops. The user interface (UI) should be simple, responsive, and intuitive, ensuring that elements like text, images, and buttons are readable and easy to interact with on smaller displays.
- **Processing Power and Memory Constraints:** Mobile devices generally have less processing power and memory compared to traditional computers. Applications must be lightweight, optimized for performance, and use minimal resources. Code efficiency is important to avoid slowdowns or crashes due to limited system capacity.
- **User Interaction Methods:** Mobile devices primarily rely on touch-based interfaces, but they may also use voice commands, gestures, and even wearables. Designers must account for these various input methods and ensure that the application responds correctly to taps, swipes, and voice inputs.
- **Context Awareness:** Mobile computing often involves context-aware applications that can adjust based on user location, time, and environmental conditions. For instance, mobile apps can offer location-based services, change settings based on the time of day, or activate certain features when entering specific locations.
- **Security and Privacy:** Mobile devices are more prone to theft, loss, and hacking, so designing secure systems is essential. Data encryption, secure authentication, and privacy considerations are important to protect user information, especially when dealing with sensitive data such as banking or healthcare applications.
- **Adaptability and Responsiveness:** The design should be adaptable to various mobile platforms (Android, iOS, Windows) and different device types (smartphones, tablets). Applications should also be responsive to different orientations (portrait and landscape) and adjust the layout accordingly.
- **Data Synchronization:** Mobile devices often need to sync data with cloud servers or other devices. Efficient synchronization mechanisms must be incorporated to ensure that data is up-to-date across devices without consuming excessive bandwidth or processing power.
- **Scalability and Upgradability:** Mobile applications should be designed with scalability in mind, allowing them to handle an increasing number of users or features without compromising performance. The ability to upgrade the app seamlessly without disrupting user experience is also a key consideration.

(b) Write a short note on Smart Appliances. 10

Answer: Smart appliances are everyday household or commercial devices that have been enhanced with advanced technologies like internet connectivity, automation, and artificial intelligence (AI) to improve their functionality and ease of use. These appliances can be controlled remotely through smartphones, tablets, or voice assistants, making them an integral part of smart homes and IoT (Internet of Things) ecosystems.

Key Features of Smart Appliances:

- **Remote Control and Monitoring:** Smart appliances can be controlled remotely using mobile apps. For example, users can turn on/off devices, adjust settings, or monitor performance while away from home. This is common in smart thermostats, washing machines, and ovens.
- **Automation:** Many smart appliances can be programmed to perform tasks automatically. For instance, a smart coffee machine can start brewing coffee at a specific time in the morning, or smart lights can turn on based on motion detection or time schedules.
- **Energy Efficiency:** Smart appliances often come with energy-saving features, allowing users to monitor and optimize their energy consumption. Smart refrigerators and air conditioners, for example, can adjust their operation based on usage patterns or external temperatures to save energy.
- **Voice Control Integration:** Most smart appliances are compatible with voice assistants like Amazon Alexa, Google Assistant, or Apple's Siri. This allows users to control appliances with simple voice commands, enhancing convenience and accessibility.
- **Data Collection and Analysis:** These appliances collect usage data and analyse it to offer insights on how to improve efficiency. For example, a smart oven might recommend cooking settings based on past preferences, or a smart washing machine might suggest the most efficient wash cycle for the current load.
- **Connectivity and Integration:** Smart appliances are part of a larger IoT network, enabling them to communicate with other smart devices in the home. This integration can result in coordinated actions, such as smart lights dimming when the TV is turned on for a movie.

- **Notifications and Alerts:** Smart appliances can send notifications and alerts to the user's phone. For example, a smart fridge can notify when food is running low or a smart washing machine can alert when the laundry cycle is complete

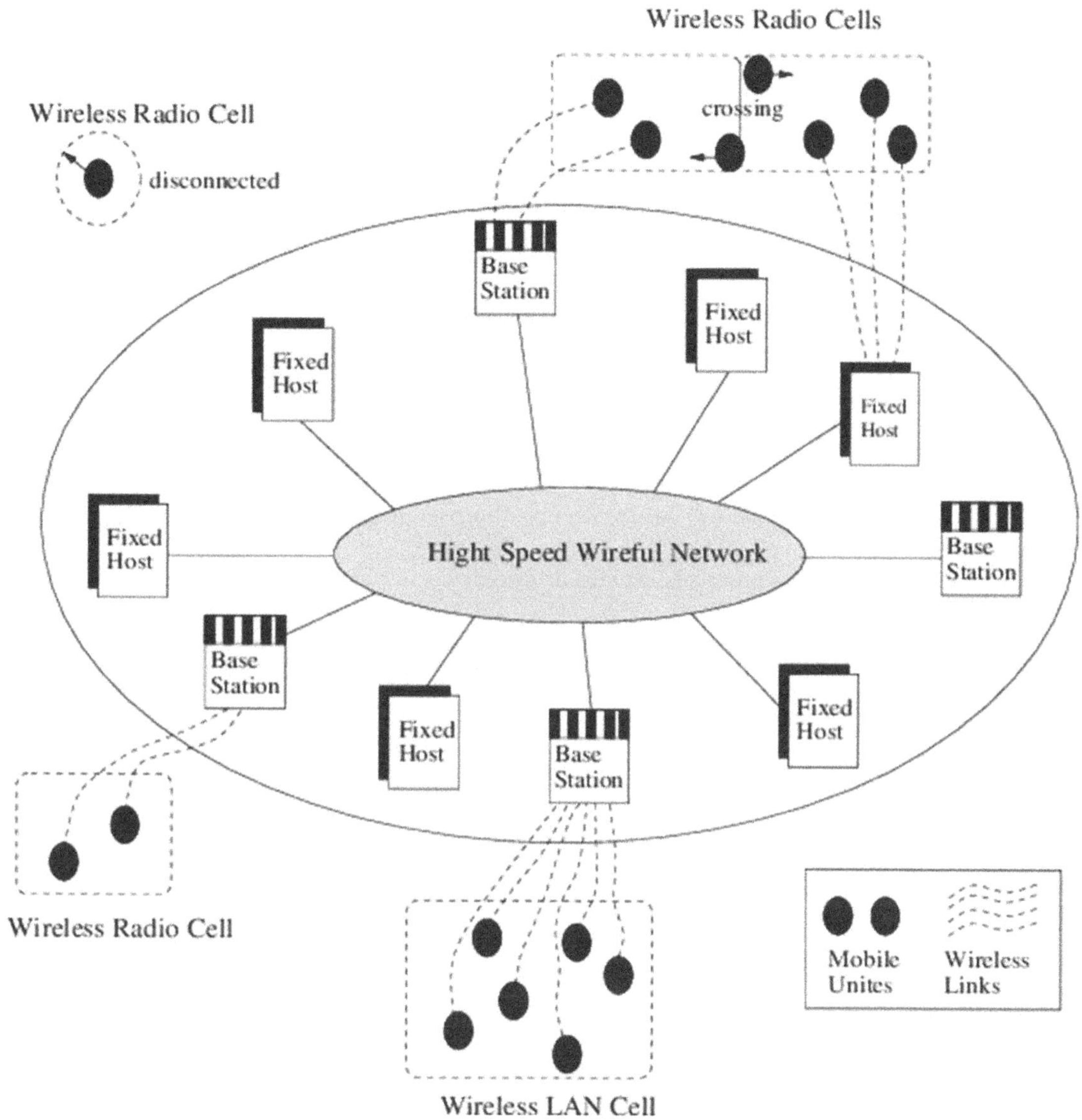

Additional Unsolved Question Paper
University of Delhi
MCS-231
Master In Computer Application (MCA)
Chapter 4: Term-End Examination, December, 2023
MCS-231: Mobile Computing

Time: 3 Hours
Maximum Marks: 100
Note: Question No. 1 is compulsory and carries 40 marks. Attempt any three questions from the rest.

Question 1 4x10=40
Define Mobile Computing. What are its primary components and applications?
a. Explain Frequency Division Multiple Access (FDMA) and its advantages, disadvantages, and applications.
b. What is Bluetooth technology? Describe its architecture and applications in mobile computing.
c. Explain the role of middleware in mobile computing. List its essential functionalities and provide examples of middleware platforms.

Question 2 2x10=20
a. Describe the architecture of the Global System for Mobile Communications (GSM) network. How does it handle calls and data?
b. What is Wi-Fi? Discuss its features, protocols, and the differences between Wi-Fi 5 and Wi-Fi 6.

Question 3 2x10=20
a. Draw and explain the Android architecture stack. Briefly discuss the role of each layer.
b. What are the main features of the iOS operating system? How does it differ from Android in terms of security and app development?

Question 4 2x10=20
a. What is Mobile IP? Explain its importance in managing mobility in networks.
b. Explain the difference between guided and unguided media in data transmission, with examples of each.

Question 5 2x10=20
a. Discuss the concept of Mobile Cloud Computing (MCC). What are its advantages and challenges?
b. What is Code Division Multiple Access (CDMA)? Explain how it differs from GSM in terms of technology and applications.

Question 6 2x10=20
a. Describe the various types of antennas used in mobile networks. What factors affect the choice of antenna?
b. What are the key features of the 5G network? Explain how it improves upon 4G technology in terms of speed, latency, and applications.

University of Delhi
MCS-231
Master In Computer Application (MCA)
Chapter 5: Term-End Examination, June, 2023
MCS-231: Mobile Computing

Time: 3 Hours
Maximum Marks: 100
Note: Question No. 1 is compulsory and carries 40 marks. Attempt any three questions from the rest.

Question 1 4x10=40

a. Explain the architecture and key components of mobile computing. Describe its applications in different sectors.
b. What is Code Division Multiple Access (CDMA)? Discuss its advantages, disadvantages, and differences from Frequency Division Multiple Access (FDMA).
c. Define mobile middleware and its role in mobile application development. List and explain common features of middleware platforms.
d. What is Long-Term Evolution (LTE)? Describe its main features and improvements over previous generations of mobile networks.

Question 2 2x10=20

a. Explain the importance of handoff and roaming in mobile networks. Describe the process and challenges associated with seamless handoff.
b. Define Near Field Communication (NFC). Discuss its applications and limitations in mobile payments and information sharing.

Question 3 2x10=20

a. Describe the architecture of the 5G network. What are its core technologies, and how do they enhance performance?
b. Explain the difference between symmetric and asymmetric encryption. Discuss the importance of encryption in mobile communication security.

Question 4 2x10=20

a. What is Zigbee technology? Explain its features, applications, and differences from Bluetooth in the context of mobile computing.
b. Describe the concept of mobile positioning. What are the various techniques used for location tracking in mobile networks?

Question 5 2x10=20

a. Explain the concept of Mobile IP. Discuss its importance and challenges in supporting mobility across networks.
b. What are mobile ad hoc networks (MANETs)? Discuss their applications, advantages, and limitations in mobile computing.

Question 6 2x10=20

a. Describe the characteristics and advantages of satellite communication in mobile networks.
b. What is Bluetooth Low Energy (BLE)? Explain its applications in IoT and how it differs from standard Bluetooth technology.

Mostly Asked Questions

1. What is Mobile Computing?

Mobile computing is a technology that enables the transmission of data, voice, and video using a wireless device without the need for a fixed physical connection. It combines mobility, wireless communication, and portability.

2. What are the components of Mobile Computing?

The components include mobile communication (e.g., GSM, CDMA, Wi-Fi), mobile hardware (e.g., smartphones, tablets), and mobile software (e.g., Android, iOS applications).

3. What are the advantages of Mobile Computing?

Advantages include portability, real-time access to data, improved productivity, and enhanced collaboration.

4. What are the disadvantages of Mobile Computing?

Disadvantages include security risks, dependence on battery power, network instability, and the cost of devices and data plans.

5. What is the difference between wireless and mobile computing?

Wireless computing refers to communication without wires, while mobile computing refers to performing computing tasks on portable devices like smartphones and laptops.

6. What is a Mobile Ad Hoc Network (MANET)?

A MANET is a self-configuring network of mobile devices connected without any fixed infrastructure or centralized administration.

7. Explain handoff in mobile communication.

Handoff is the process of transferring an ongoing call or data session from one base station to another as the user moves between coverage areas.

8. What are the types of handoffs?

There are two types: hard handoff (break-before-make) and soft handoff (make-before-break).

9. What is GSM?

GSM (Global System for Mobile Communications) is a standard for 2G digital cellular networks that allows mobile communication over large areas.

10. What are the services provided by GSM?

GSM provides services such as voice calls, SMS (Short Message Service), and data services like GPRS/EDGE.

11. What is GPRS?

GPRS (General Packet Radio Service) is a packet-switched mobile data service on 2G and 3G networks, used for internet access and MMS.

12. What is the difference between GSM and CDMA?

GSM uses SIM cards and TDMA/FDMA technologies, whereas CDMA does not use SIM cards and uses code division multiplexing.

13. What are mobile IP and its purpose?

Mobile IP allows mobile devices to move across networks while maintaining the same IP address, ensuring seamless internet connectivity.

14. What is WAP?

WAP (Wireless Application Protocol) is a suite of protocols allowing mobile devices to access information over wireless networks.

15. What is Bluetooth and its applications?

Bluetooth is a short-range wireless technology used for file sharing, wireless audio devices, IoT connections, and more.

16. What are the features of 4G mobile networks?

4G offers high-speed internet up to 100 Mbps, supports HD video streaming, and provides IP-based voice and data services.

17. What is 5G and how is it different from 4G?

5G provides ultra-fast speeds (up to 10 Gbps), ultra-low latency (<1 ms), and massive IoT support, making it significantly better than 4G.

18. What is mobile security and why is it important?

Mobile security involves protecting mobile devices from threats like malware and unauthorized access. It is important due to the sensitive personal and business data stored on mobile devices.

19. Explain the term mobile agent.

A mobile agent is a software program that can migrate across devices or networks and perform tasks autonomously.

20. What are some applications of Mobile Computing?

Applications include mobile banking, e-commerce, GPS navigation, telemedicine, and online education.

21. What is mobile IP tunneling?

Mobile IP tunneling is the process of encapsulating data packets to send them from a home agent to a foreign agent while maintaining the same IP address for the mobile device.

22. What is the difference between mobile computing and wireless networking?

Mobile computing focuses on mobility of devices and computing on the go, while wireless networking is about enabling communication between devices without physical cables.

23. What is a base station in mobile communication?

A base station is a fixed point of communication in a mobile network that connects mobile devices to the network using radio waves.

24. What is HLR in GSM architecture?

HLR (Home Location Register) is a database in GSM networks that stores information about subscribers, including their location and services subscribed.

25. What is VLR in GSM architecture?

VLR (Visitor Location Register) is a temporary database that stores information about subscribers currently roaming in a particular area.

26. What are the challenges in mobile computing?

Challenges include limited bandwidth, network congestion, device battery constraints, and ensuring security and privacy.

27. What is the difference between mobility and portability?

Mobility refers to the ability to access network resources while moving, while portability is the ability to carry a device from one location to another.

28. What is a cell in mobile communication?

A cell is a geographical area covered by a base station in a mobile network, allowing efficient frequency reuse.

29. What is the difference between microcells, macrocells, and picocells?

Macrocells cover large areas, microcells cover smaller areas within macrocells, and picocells are used indoors for very small coverage.

30. What is the purpose of a SIM card?

A SIM (Subscriber Identity Module) card securely stores subscriber information and enables authentication on mobile networks.

31. What is a mobile hotspot?

A mobile hotspot is a feature that allows a device to share its cellular data connection with other devices over Wi-Fi.

32. What is TDMA in mobile communication?

TDMA (Time Division Multiple Access) is a channel access method where users share the same frequency by dividing it into different time slots.

33. What is FDMA in mobile communication?

FDMA (Frequency Division Multiple Access) assigns different frequency bands to multiple users for communication.

34. What is CDMA in mobile communication?

CDMA (Code Division Multiple Access) allows multiple users to share the same frequency using unique codes for each user.

35. What is LTE?

LTE (Long Term Evolution) is a 4G wireless broadband technology that provides high-speed data and supports IP-based communication.

36. What are the benefits of LTE?

Benefits include high data rates, low latency, and improved capacity for handling more users simultaneously.

37. What is a femtocell?

A femtocell is a small cellular base station used in homes or offices to improve mobile network coverage indoors.

38. What is QoS in mobile computing?

QoS (Quality of Service) refers to the performance level of a service, ensuring priorities like bandwidth, latency, and error rates are met.

39. What is mobile cloud computing?

Mobile cloud computing is the combination of cloud computing and mobile networks, allowing users to access and run applications on cloud infrastructure via mobile devices.

40. What is the difference between 2G, 3G, 4G, and 5G networks?

2G introduced digital communication, 3G enabled data and multimedia, 4G focused on high-speed internet, and 5G offers ultra-fast speeds and low latency for advanced applications.

41. What are wearable computing devices?

Wearable computing devices are electronic gadgets worn on the body, like smartwatches and fitness bands, providing computing and communication capabilities.

42. What is GPS and how is it used in mobile devices?

GPS (Global Positioning System) is a satellite-based navigation system that provides location and time information to mobile devices.

43. What is mobile VPN?

A mobile VPN extends secure access to a private network for mobile devices over public internet connections.

44. What is mobile middleware?

Mobile middleware is software that connects mobile applications with backend services or databases, handling communication, security, and data synchronization.

45. What are the different types of mobile operating systems?

Examples include Android, iOS, Windows Phone, and HarmonyOS.

46. What is NFC and how is it used?

NFC (Near Field Communication) is a short-range wireless technology used for contactless payments and data exchange between devices.

47. What is an SMS gateway?

An SMS gateway is a service that enables sending and receiving SMS messages from a computer to a mobile device.

48. What is MMS?

MMS (Multimedia Messaging Service) is a standard that allows sending multimedia content like images, audio, and video through mobile networks.

49. What is mobile commerce (m-commerce)?

Mobile commerce refers to buying and selling goods or services using mobile devices over wireless networks.

50. What is BYOD in mobile computing?

BYOD (Bring Your Own Device) is a policy where employees use their personal mobile devices for accessing company resources.

Printed at Repro India Ltd.